MW00851680

Kumihimo Endings: The finishing touch for every braid © Pru McRae

ISBN: 978-1-9164130-0-9

www.prumihimo.com

Published in 2018 by Prumihimo Publishing

Photography © Michael Wicks
www.michaelwicks.com

All rights reserved. No part of this book may be reproduced, stored in a retrieval system, or transmitted in any form or by any means, electronic, mechanical, photocopying, recording or otherwise, without the prior written permission of Pru McRae. No part of this book may be taught or copied and distributed as class handouts without the direct permission of the author. As a professional Prumihimo® artist, designer and teacher, Pru McRae is available to share her ideas with your craft group or class and may be contacted via her website prumihimo.com

If you do find any errors or you have any questions, please contact me via prumihimo.com as I would be delighted to have the opportunity to make corrections in the next print run. Please note, this book has been written using the UK English spelling of words such as: colour, neighbour, practise (used as a verb only), etc.

Printed in the UK.

Contents

· · · · · · · · · ·

Introduction

Kumihimo braiding is a wonderfully relaxing and satisfying activity, and for most braiders the process is just as enjoyable as the end product. However, the same cannot be said of finishing off the ends of the braids and making the braid into a piece of jewellery or a useful item. Too many braids lie unfinished and unloved in a craft bag or at the back of a drawer! This book aims to address this problem by explaining in detail the main finishing options and expanding them with different variations. My experience of almost a decade of kumihimo braiding – for publication, broadcast and most of all for pleasure – is brought together in this book. The clear advice, coupled with clever tips and tricks, will demystify the process of creating endings and will provide a solution for every braid. I encourage you to try as many of the techniques in this book as possible to discover what works best for you, then narrow it down to four or five methods that you can turn to with confidence, time and time again.

Certain key techniques are used in many of the ending methods, so these have been grouped together in one chapter where they are explained in detail. Look for the shaded box, which indicates that expanded instructions are available in the key techniques chapter.

The majority of ending methods explained in this book can be used for either beaded braids or braids without beads. The aim is to provide as much variety and as many options as possible, so that you can mix and match different elements of a design to suit your taste. For instance, you may be making a bag charm using the knot and tassel method on page 68, but if you prefer to finish the tassel with beads, you can find those instructions on page 43. Unless otherwise specified, all the ending methods are suitable for both necklaces and bracelets.

The braids shown in this book were made using the round kumihimo disk, the square kumihimo plate and Pru McRae's unique Prumihimo® disk. Instructions for these braids and for the jewellery designs can be found either as tutorials on the Prumihimo® website (Prumihimo.com) or in videos on the Prumihimo® YouTube channel (YouTube.com/c/Prumihimo).

Planning

The best approach is to consider how a piece will be finished off before you start to braid. For some methods this is essential, because part of the fastening, such as a button or toggle, is centred on the cords at the very beginning of the braiding process. For other methods the choice of ending will affect the length of braid required: for example, separate cones, additional beads and a large toggle clasp are much longer than a simple glue-in clasp, so the braid needs to be sized to take this into account.

Six considerations when planning your ending

1. Choose the findings/materials and make sure they match the colour, size and style of the intended braid. Remember that if jump rings are required, the colour will need to match too.

2. Lay out the clasp, cones, beads, etc. in the order you want to use them, and measure the length of them. Toggle clasps often need an extra jump ring to allow them to function properly, especially if you plan to have a large bead or wide end cap close to the clasp. This needs to be taken into account.

3. Check how much of the braid will be inside the end caps; this can vary significantly. Check both end caps on a clasp because sometimes they vary in depth. The additional length to be taken into account is the length of the clasp and extras, minus the length of the braid inside the end caps.

4. If the item is being made to sell, it may be necessary to adjust the size for the customer. This is only possible with some types of endings.

5. Consider how appropriate the clasp or fastening method is for the type of jewellery. Will it be easy to operate behind the neck or with one hand?

6. Assess how the choice of ending will affect the balance of the piece. A heavyweight clasp on a necklace will pull to the front during use. On a bracelet, if the clasp is too lightweight it will pull to the upper side of the wrist.

Sizing

There are many variables involved in braiding, such as tension, thickness of cord, brand of bead, etc., so tutorials and instructions can only ever be guidelines and should not be relied on to achieve a precise length. The sizing of bracelets is particularly important because a small variation in size can make them unwearable. It is not sufficient to rely on a length measurement alone, because the thickness of a braid will significantly alter the length you need to make. A good way to check the length of braid required to make a bracelet is to balance the findings on your wrist, estimate how much of the braid will be inserted into the end cap and wrap the braid around the wrist, making sure that the fit is comfortable. If you are making for others, a bracelet sizing cone or a bracelet sizing board can be used.

Remember to stretch the braid before making a final decision on the length. All braids will stretch to a lesser or greater degree when they are first made, depending on the braid structure and your tension. It is important to give the braid one firm stretch and allow it to relax back into shape for approximately 10 minutes. If this is not done, the braid may stretch when it is worn.

It is useful to build up a comprehensive stash of findings and materials, so that you have the flexibility to create the perfect ending for any braid. Even with the best forward planning, sometimes a braid turns out differently to what was expected, so it is good to have alternatives available. It is rare for any one retailer to be able to offer all of the items you need, so be ready to purchase whenever you see something suitable. Things to look out for would include:

▶   A range of end caps in different sizes. The most useful glue-in end cap sizes have an internal diameter of 3–4mm, 5mm, 6mm and 8mm. The most useful end cones for use with wire have an internal diameter of 5–8mm and a length of 1–2cm

- ▶ 0.8mm/20 gauge wire in silver, gold, copper, etc. to match the end caps
- ▶ Strong, good-quality jump rings, with an internal diameter of 4–5mm, to match the end caps
- ▶ A range of sizes of clasp in different metals and styles
- ▶ Attractive buttons, 1.5cm–3cm in diameter
- ▶ Crimp bead covers in different metals. These are useful for concealing knots
- ▶ 4mm, 6mm and 8mm beads to top off cones
- ▶ A selection of sewing or beading thread in different colours for bindings

Equipment

The simple wirework used in some ending methods requires a set of jewellery-making pliers, which would include round-nose pliers, flat-nose or chain-nose pliers and wire cutters.

Cone-making tools, looping/bail-making pliers or stepped mandrels are used for some techniques, but it is possible to make use of household items such as pen tops, icing nozzles or knitting needles.

A useful device for measuring braids is a knitting needle sizer. This will enable you to check the fit of a braid in an end cap before buying. The internal diameter of the end cap is the important measurement here.

Strong scissors or metal shears are needed to cut through braids that have been glued and sealed. It is best to cut and shape them before the glue has fully hardened. A sharp knife and old chopping board can be used on tougher braids if necessary.

Needles are used in different ways when finishing off a braid. To make a sewn binding, it is best to use an ordinary sewing needle. When pulling cord under a binding or into the core of a braid, a strong needle with a large eye, such as a darning needle, is required.

Thread and cord burners are very useful for sealing the end of a cord or braid. A thread burner is sufficient for beading cord of all sizes and for threads, but a cord burner is required for satin cord and braids. Only synthetic materials can be used with these burners. A lighter can be used to seal and melt cord ends, but great care must be taken.

Key techniques

In this chapter you will find detailed instructions for all the most important techniques that are used time and time again to create the ending methods explained in this book. It is worth practising these techniques on scrap materials first, so that you can carry them out with accuracy and with confidence on your finished jewellery. Mastering these techniques will enable you to finish off any braid to a professional standard, achieving a result which is both secure and attractive.

Removing the braid from the disk

When removing the braid from the disk, it is important to prevent the braid from unravelling. There are two equally effective ways of doing this:

1. Pinch the top of the braid from underneath the disk using the thumb and forefinger, remove the cords from the slots and quickly tie an overhand knot, making sure that the end of the braided section is caught in the knot.

2. Lift two opposite cords from the disk and tie them in a double knot. Lift two more opposite cords and tie them in a double knot. This should be enough to stabilise the braid, but for extra security this process can be repeated for the remaining two pairs of cords.

Sealing the braid

Unless otherwise specified in the instructions, all braid ends need to be sealed before the clasp or fastening is attached. This is so that the individual cords adhere together and the braid end can be cut and shaped without unravelling. A number of different products can be used for this purpose, but if a glued method of attaching end caps is going to be used, it is important to use the same product to avoid compatibility issues. If a glued method is not going to be used, the braid can be sealed with fabric glue, all-purpose glue, fray-prevention products, superglue or clear nail varnish. All of these products will have the effect of darkening or stiffening the braid, so they should be applied sparingly. Spread a small amount of glue in a band measuring approximately 1cm wide around the braid at the point where it needs to be cut. Allow the product to dry but not harden, so that the braid can be cut and shaped. If the end cap you plan to use is a snug fit on the braid, it is possible to decrease the thickness of the braid slightly at this point. While the glue is still pliable, stretch the braid firmly and keep it stretched until the glue sets. Conversely, the braid can be made slightly wider by compressing it from both ends.

▶ **Please remember to read the manufacturer's safety instructions carefully before using any sort of glue.**

Cutting, trimming and shaping the braid

Strong kitchen scissors or metal shears are best for cutting through glued braids, or a sharp knife and chopping board can be used. The best time to cut the braid is when the glue has dried, but is not yet hard. After cutting through the braid, roll the cut end between the thumb and forefinger to compress and neaten the cut edge. Try it for size in the ending you plan to use. If you intend to use the wire method to attach the end cap, the fit is less important, but for the glue method it is essential to have a good fit. Some endings are conical in shape or have tapered ends, so the braid can be trimmed to the right shape, as long as you only cut through the glued part of the braid.

Wire techniques

Equipment – a set of jewellery-making pliers, including round-nose pliers, flat or chain-nose pliers and wire cutters

When working with wire, it is important to be aware of safety considerations. Wire can be sharp and springy, while cut ends can fly across the room at speed, so make sure your eyes and hands are protected and that you work well away from other people or pets.

For all the wire techniques described below, 0.8mm/20 gauge wire has been used, because while it is strong, it is also easy to work with. Other thicknesses or gauges of wire can be used, but thinner wires will be less durable and thicker wires will be harder to work with.

The precise amount of wire required can vary considerably, depending on the thickness of the braid, so the lengths suggested here can be only an approximation. It is good practice to keep records of what works for you when you try something for the first time, so that you can adjust the quantity the next time you try a technique.

Wrapped loop

This is probably the most useful wire technique of all because it is both a strong and a decorative connection that can be used in so many ways. Even if your first efforts are not very neat, your loops will definitely improve with practice.

1. Grip the wire with the round-nose pliers close to the cone or bead. The part of the pliers used to grip the wire will determine how many wraps will be needed to finish the loop. If the narrowest part of the pliers is used to grip the wire, just one or two wraps will fit in. If the widest part of the pliers is used, four or five wraps will fit in.

2. Pull the wire towards you to create a right angle (a bend of 90 degrees).

3. Change the grip on the wire so that one arm of the pliers is above the bend in the wire and the other is below the bend in the wire. Wrap the wire around the top arm to form three-quarters of a circle.

4. Change the grip on the wire so that one arm is in the loop and the other is above it. Wrap the wire around the bottom arm of the pliers to complete the circle, and then wrap it neatly around the stem of the loop, as many times as necessary to fill the gap between the loop and the bead.

5. Keeping one arm of the pliers in the loop, straighten the loop so that it sits in the centre above the wire. Trim the wire close to the wrap and use flat-nose pliers to squash the cut end down, so that it does not protrude.

Flat spiral

This technique is a good way of giving a decorative finish to wire.

1. Grip the wire 1mm from the end with round-nose pliers. Turn the pliers to create a semicircle. The very end of the wire will be flat. Cut off this flat part.

2. Grip the wire with the tip of the round-nose pliers and turn the pliers to create a full circle and then a further half circle.

3. Switch to flat-nose pliers and grip the spiral. Turn the pliers to build the spiral to the desired size.

Double spiral and wrap

Several ending techniques use a wire wrap finished off with flat spirals to join two braids. For evenly sized spirals it is necessary to measure and mark the wire. Use a non-permanent marker pen, so that the marking can be wiped off at the end. The length of wire required will vary according to the size of the braid, the size of the spirals and the number of wraps. Practise with 15cm of wire.

1. Measure the wire and make a mark to indicate where the first spiral should end. For a small spiral 2cm is required, 3cm for a medium spiral and 4–5cm for a large spiral.

2. Create the first spiral as in the instructions for the flat spiral. Stop winding when the mark on the wire is reached.

3. Hold the spiral so that the mark is in the centre of the braids. Wrap the wire around the braids several times as evenly as possible. Do not wrap too firmly or the wire will compress the braid and it will then be more difficult to make the wraps even.

4. Measure the wire from the middle of the braids and cut the wire to create the size of spiral required.

5. Create the second spiral as in the instructions for the flat spiral, finishing so that it sits neatly opposite the first spiral.

Coil

This technique is best done on looping pliers because they are used to grip the wire firmly at the beginning. If looping pliers are not available, knitting needles are a reasonable alternative because they come in a range of sizes. Use some pliers to hold the wire against the knitting needle at the start.

1. If possible, work from the reel of wire to avoid waste. Grip the wire close to the end with the looping pliers and turn the pliers, feeding the wire with the other hand. To keep turning the pliers you will need to keep changing your grip. It is important to turn the pliers, rather than wrapping the wire around them, in order to avoid twisting the wire.

2. Continue to turn until the coil is just longer than required. The first ring is often not as tight as the following ones, so it can be snipped off. Make sure that the cut ends of the wire at the top and bottom are on the same side of the coil.

Jump rings

Jump rings are used frequently to attach clasps and join sections of a design, so it is important to know how to use them correctly.

1. To open the ring, grip it on either side of the join with pliers and twist your hands in opposite directions so that the ends of the ring slide past each other, thus opening the ring while retaining its shape.

2. To close the ring, use the same action. If necessary, you can twist the ring to and fro several times to bring the ends as close as possible.

Knots

Two simple knots are used frequently in this book. Sometimes a knot is temporary, so it should only be lightly tightened to enable it to be undone easily later. A permanent knot needs to be tightened as much as possible. When knotting a group of cords, each cord can be tightened individually.

Overhand knot

Hold the cord and form a loop. Bring one cord through the loop and tighten.

Double knot

There are several variations of knots with a double construction, such as granny knots, reef knots and square knots. Any of these can be used. Cross the cords and pass one end under. Cross the cords again, pass one cord under and then tighten. If a larger knot is required, repeat the process.

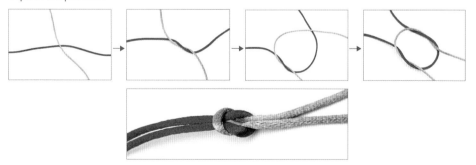

Knotting and sealing the end of a cord

This technique is often used at the end of tassels. There are three ways of creating a neat finish. The heat methods involve melting the cord, so they can only be used with synthetic cords. Check on a scrap piece of cord first to make sure that it will melt. Great care needs to be taken when using a naked flame or a thread/cord burner.

Glue method

Tie a knot in the cord and tighten it very firmly. Seal the knot with a drop of glue. Products with brushes or precision nozzles are easiest to use for this purpose. Otherwise a cocktail stick or piece of wire can be used to pick up small amounts of glue to apply to the knot. When the glue has set but not hardened, trim the cord end close to the knot.

Lighter method

Tie a knot in the cord and tighten it very firmly. Trim the cord approximately 1mm from the knot. Bring the flame close to the cord, using the lower, blue part of the flame to avoid blackening the cord. The heat of the flame will cause the cord to retreat towards the knot and form a small blob at the end. Do not allow the cord to touch the flame or catch fire. After the cord has cooled down completely, apply a small amount of glue to the knot for extra security.

Thread or cord burner method

Tie a knot in the cord and tighten it very firmly. For thin cords such as beading cord, a thread burner can be used. For thicker cords such as satin cord, a cord burner is required. Use the burner to cut through the cord close to the knot. It will cut and seal the end of the cord. After the cord has cooled down completely, apply a small amount of glue to the knot for extra security.

Simple start – starting a braid from a ring, button, toggle or other finding

A very discreet start to a braid can be made by attaching the cords directly to a finding. The important point to remember with this method is that the cords will be folded in half and passed through the finding, so you will need half the number of cords, but double the length for each cord.

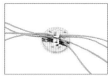

1. Thread all the cords through the ring and centre the ring on the cords.

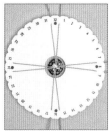

2. Hold the cords firmly in the ring and position the cords on the disk as required. Make sure that the cords are not pulled too tightly at this stage or they may pull through the ring and the ends will be uneven. Each cord should be positioned straight across the disk in diagonally opposite slots.

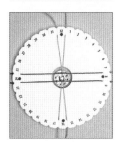

3. Start to braid. At this point you still need to be very careful not to pull too hard on the cords and you may need to hold the finding in the middle of the hole in the disk. After each cord has been moved once, it will be firmly fixed.

Note: It may not be possible to pass all the cords through the ring you are using. In this case pass through as many as you can and position those cords on the disk. Then lay the other cords across the disk and into the appropriate slots. Start to braid using the cords through the ring first. After all the cords have been moved once, the additional cords will be firmly worked into the braid.

Binding

This is a very useful technique that can be used to joint two braids, to secure a braid to make a tassel or to reinforce a braid for extra security before attaching an ending using glue or wire. It gives the opportunity to use a different type of cord or thread to create the binding. This can either be to make the binding as invisible as possible by using a very thin thread in a matching colour, or to make a feature of the binding by using a contrasting colour or a sparkly thread. Beading thread, Fireline or good-quality sewing thread are all good materials for bindings.

1. Thread a needle with the chosen thread and sew through the braid, leaving a tail of 5cm. Sew back through the braid several times until the thread is firmly secured in the braid. The stitches will be least visible if they pierce the braid in between the cords. Give the thread a firm tug to make sure that there is absolutely no slippage.

2. Wind the thread tightly around the braid, covering the stitching as neatly as possible. The thread needs to be wound around the braid six to eight times to keep it firm, but for decorative purposes it can be wound around as many times as you like.

3. Sew through the braid several times as before, keeping a firm grip on the binding to prevent it unwinding, until the thread is firmly secured. Keep the stitches as close as possible to the binding to keep them invisible. If the braid on one side of the binding is going to be unravelled, it is important to make sure that these stitches are on the opposite side of the binding.

4. Trim the thread ends close to the braid to create a tidy finish. Alternatively, the needle can be used to pass the thread under the binding. A drop of glue can be added to the binding for extra security and this is advised, especially for slippery cords. The glue may darken the cord, but as long as it is only applied sparingly to the binding and not allowed to seep up the braid underneath, it will not be unsightly and it will ensure that the binding does not slip or come undone. Brush-on superglue or fray-prevention products are easy to use for this purpose. If the braid on one side of the binding is going to be unravelled, it is best to apply the glue immediately after doing this.

A few words about glue

Glue is used for two different purposes in finishing off kumihimo ends and it is important to know which type of glue to use for each purpose. Throughout this book glue is referred to as either general glue or strong glue. If the type of glue is not specified, either will be suitable. Which brand to use is a matter of personal choice depending on how you like to work. Prices can vary considerably and some people may find some glue odours offensive. Some glues are available with fine nozzles or brushes to make them easier to apply. For glues that have no applicator, a cocktail stick or scrap length of wire can be used to apply small amounts of glue with precision. Try different glues to see which work best for you.

It is important to stress that when using any type of glue the manufacturer's instructions and safety guidelines should be read carefully and observed. Make sure you protect yourself and all surfaces as well as ensuring good ventilation while you work. Never allow glues to be used near children, animals or food.

General glue

This is used for sealing and stiffening braids and for adding extra security to knots and bindings. For these uses the glue needs to be able to be absorbed by the fibres of the cord. It also needs to dry fairly fast to a clear and firm finish. A wide range of products can be used. These include:

▶ **all-purpose glue**: this is a very reasonably priced and versatile adhesive, which seals knots and bindings very effectively. It can also be used together with crimps and fold-over endings. It tends to be rather free-flowing from the tube and can become stringy and messy.

- ▶ **fabric glue**: this comes in many different formulations, so it is difficult to generalise about this type of glue. The easiest to use are those where the tubes have small nozzles.
- ▶ **superglue with a brush**: this is very convenient for sealing knots and bindings. It is strong enough to use with both crimps and fold-over endings. Extra care needs to be taken because it is very fast acting and can bond flesh together or to other materials.
- ▶ **fray-prevention products**: these can be used to seal knots, bindings and braid ends, but are not strong enough for other purposes.
- ▶ **clear nail polish**: this is a very cost-effective and convenient way to seal knots and bindings. It is not an adhesive, so it is not strong enough for other purposes.

All of these glues will have the effect of darkening and stiffening the braid or cord to a greater or lesser extent, depending on the type of cord and where it is applied. It is wise to test the glue on a scrap length of cord before using it on a piece of work. When applying glue to a binding, be sparing with the glue so that it sinks into the binding and the braid underneath, but does not travel up the braid.

Strong glue

This is used to stick end caps onto a braid. It needs to be extremely strong and suitable for use with both fibres and metal. It can be hazardous to mix different types of glue, so the same glue also needs to be used to seal the braid. There are various different glues available, but the three most popular strong glues used by the kumihimo community are:

- ▶ **2-part epoxy**: this glue is fast becoming the most popular glue among kumihimo braiders. Be sure to select the clear, fast-acting formula, which is very strong and easy to use. It is necessary to mix the two parts of the glue together, and the brands which come in two separate tubes are more convenient than those which come in a double syringe. This glue sets in 3–5 minutes, which allows a reasonable time to get the fit right. It should be cured for 24 hours, or as recommended by the manufacturer. An exact fit is not required for this glue because it will fill in the spaces.
- ▶ **clear jewellery glue, such as E6000**: this glue has always been a popular choice of adhesive among jewellery makers, but it does take a long time to set and needs to be left to cure for several days. Some brands may not be available worldwide because they

are banned in some countries and states because they contain certain chemicals. A good fit between the braid and the end is required for this glue to work.

▶ **gel-style superglue**: this glue is very fast acting, so you have to act quickly and with great care. It forms a very strong bond when used correctly, but it can become brittle over time and if too much is used, a white 'bloom' may appear on the outside of metal findings. A good fit between the braid and the end is required for this glue.

Alternatives to using glue

Glue is used freely in this book, but if you have a strong aversion to glue, it can be avoided. In most cases where an ending is glued on, it could be attached with wire as long as suitable end cones or caps are used. Glue is widely used to seal the end of braids, but there are two alternatives to this: either bind the braid very tightly, close to the end, so the individual cords do not spread out, or, for synthetic cords, use a cord burner to cut through the end of the braid, which will fuse the cords together. It is often advised to use glue to seal bindings as an extra level of security, but except for very slippery cords, this is not essential as long as the thread is very tightly bound around the braid. Knots can be sealed with a cord burner or a naked flame, or a few tiny stitches can be used to keep them tight.

Glued endings

Attaching an end cap to a braid using glue is the most widespread and popular way to finish it and make it into a piece of jewellery. The reason for this is that it is straightforward and does not require specialist skills. However, using the correct technique and the most appropriate glue is essential to avoid the disappointment of the end cap coming off over time or during wear. A really strong and reliable bond is required for sticking the end cap onto a braid and the glue must be suitable for both the fibres of the braid and the material of the end cap, which is usually metal. The three most popular types of glue, due to their reliability, ease of use and availability, are 2-part epoxy, E6000 and gel superglue, and more information about them can be found in the chapter on glue.

It is important to stress that, when using any type of glue, the manufacturer's instructions and safety guidelines should be read carefully and observed. Make sure you protect yourself and all surfaces, and work in an area with good ventilation.

Findings

A beautiful and varied range of glue-in findings are available. Some are fastened with magnets, some have integrated hook and eye fastenings, while others need to have a separate clasp attached with jump rings. Look for deep glue-in sections, which offer the greatest security. Magnets need to be strong to stand up to wear, especially for bracelets. The strongest bonds will be formed when the braid is a good fit in the end cap, which should have an internal diameter that is approximately 1–2mm greater than the diameter of the braid.

Master technique for the glued ending method

Before the braid end can be glued into the finding, it needs to be sealed with glue and trimmed. It is important to use the same glue for sealing the braid as you intend to use to attach it to the finding, to avoid compatibility problems.

Materials – cones, caps or clasps that can be used with glue, wet wipes ready for clean-ups.

1. Spread a small amount of glue in a band measuring approximately 1cm wide around the braid at the point where it needs to be cut. Allow the glue to dry but not harden, and cut though the glued section of the braid with strong scissors or a knife. The glue should still be malleable, so roll the end of the braid between the thumb and forefinger to compress and neaten the cut edge. The braid can now be trimmed and shaped to fit the end cap without fear of it unravelling.

2. Try the braid in the finding, assessing how much space is available for glue. It is best to be sparing with glue because it is unsightly if it is allowed to squeeze out of the sides of the end cap or travel up the braid, as it will darken and stiffen the braid. Make sure the finding is clean and free of dust.

3. Use a cocktail stick to pick up a small amount of glue and apply it to the inside of the finding. Apply a small drop of glue to the end of the braid.

4. Insert the braid into the finding using a twisting motion to spread the glue. If you have used too much glue and it is overflowing, remove the braid immediately and wipe off the excess glue from the braid and the finding. Try again with less glue.

5. Leave the glue to dry and cure for at least the full time recommended by the manufacturer. Do not be tempted to check or move the braid during this time because this will compromise the bond. Do not leave the two parts of a clasp joined together while the glue dries and cures in case any glue has escaped onto the clasp. This is particularly important for barrel-style magnetic clasps because there are sometimes tiny gaps between the magnet and the barrel through which glue can seep. Weather conditions, such as cold and humidity, can affect the time it takes for glue to dry, so try to protect the piece from extremes.

Double braids with magnetic clasps

Sourcing a clasp for a double-braid bracelet can be difficult and an effective solution is to use two magnetic clasps. As long as the clasps are correctly lined up, they will pull the two braids together and sit neatly. They will also benefit from the double security of two clasps.

Materials – 2 cylindrical magnetic clasps.

1. Put the two clasps together so that they attract each other and will sit side by side. It is very easy to mix them up and if they are not correctly lined up, they will repel each other. Therefore, be careful to separate the clasps and lay them out on the work surface so that you can clearly see which end needs to go on which braid.

2. Glue the endings on, one by one. Close the bracelet to check that the clasps lock together. Leave the bracelet to dry and cure in the open position.

Safety chains

Magnetic clasps are very easy to use and have a sleek appearance, but they are not as secure as most other clasps. This is more of a problem for bracelets than necklaces and the best solution is to use a safety chain. For thinner braids the chain can be attached with jump rings after the clasp has been attached, but for wider braids the jump rings need to be threaded onto the braid before the clasp is attached to avoid distorting the rings.

Materials – glue-in magnetic clasp, 10cm chain, 2 large jump rings.

1. Measure the diameter of the end of the braid and select two jump rings with an internal diameter approximately 2–3mm larger than the braid.

2. Work with one end of the braid at a time. Attach one end of a piece of chain measuring approximately 8–10cm to one jump ring. Slide the ring onto the braid. Use masking tape to hold the ring in position and to keep it away from the glue and the magnet. Glue the braid into the magnetic clasp, as before.

3. Check the length of the chain by holding it around the widest part of your hand. It needs to be long enough so that the bracelet can just slip over the knuckles. Cut the chain to the required length and attach the free end of the chain to the second jump ring.

4. Slide the ring onto the other end of the braid. Use masking tape to hold the ring in position and to keep it away from the glue. Glue the braid into the other part of the magnetic clasp.

Customisation

While you can achieve a sleek and streamlined look with many of the integrated clasps, there are times when you may wish to give your work a rather more personal finishing touch. Here are a few ideas.

Patina paints

These paints have been designed to be used with finished metal and they are a great way to add your own personality to the endings of your piece of jewellery. They are also a way of solving the problem of not having a clasp in the correct metal colour. The paints are usually sold in sets of three colours to replicate distressed or organic effects, such as verdigris or rust. Simply dab on the colours in rough, overlapping patches to build up the colour to create the desired effect. A nail file can be used to remove some layers of paint to give the appearance of wear. Protect the surface with several coats of compatible varnish, but be aware that over time the distressed effect will increase, especially where metal parts touch during use.

Beaded sleeve

A basic knowledge of peyote stitch is required for this method. Conceal simple magnetic tube clasps with a sleeve of peyote stitch. The rectangle of bead stitching needs to be a snug fit around the barrel of the clasp. It is easy to adjust the dimensions to fit different sizes of clasp.

Materials – cylindrical magnetic clasps, size 11 seed beads, beading thread and needle.

1. Attach both ends of the clasp as described in the instructions for the glued ending master technique.

2. Create a rectangle of peyote stitch. For the 6mm internal diameter clasp used in the example, the peyote rectangle was made with size 11 beads, starting with eight beads, so that there are four beads in both of the first two rows and 26 rows in total. The exact number of beads and rows needed will depend on the size of the clasp used. The beading needs to fit snugly around the clasp.

3. Apply a very small amount of glue to one side of the clasp and wrap the beading around the clasp. Brush-on superglue is very easy to use for this. An alternative method is to use double-sided tape around the clasp.

4. Stitch the ends of the rectangle of beading together. The tail of the thread can be used to sew the sleeve onto the braid, by sewing right through the braid and the beading several times close to the edge of the clasp.

Wired endings

Using wire to attach an end cone and clasp is a very attractive and secure fastening method and only very basic wire-working skills are required. A highly customised look is achievable because the covering for the end of the braid and the clasp are separate and there is the opportunity to add on beads or charms to create your own style. It is possible to create many different sorts of covering, such as end cones, wire wraps and beads. The other advantage of this type of ending is that a precise fit of the braid in the cone or cap is not necessary.

Wire

A range of gauges of wire can be used and your choice will depend on personal preference and/or what you have available. I recommend 0.8mm wire, which is 20 gauge, because it is strong yet easy to work with and will fit through most beads. It is also possible to use 0.6mm/22 gauge wire, but this will not be quite as strong. For greater strength 1mm/18 gauge wire can be used, but this is a little harder to work with and will not fit through smaller beads.

When working with wire, make sure you protect your eyes and hands from sharp points.

Binding

If the braid has large or heavy beads close to the ends it is a good idea to use a binding in addition to sealing the braid, to prevent the beads from working loose. Bind the braid before it is sealed, so that the binding is glued to the braid.

Master technique for the wired ending method

End cones are readily available in many different styles, sizes and materials. They are also known as bead cones, bead caps or kumihimo cones.

Materials – end cones, wire, 2 beads (optional), jump rings and clasp.

Equipment – wire cutters, round-nose pliers, flat/chain-nose pliers, cork.

1. Start with a sealed and trimmed braid. Cut 10cm of wire. Pierce the braid with the wire close to the glued part. The wire should not be visible in the final design, so make sure that it will be covered by the cone. Use a cork or something similar to protect your hands when you push the sharp wire through the braid. If the braid is very tight, it may be difficult to get the wire though. If so, make a hole first with an ordinary sewing needle, then stretch the hole with a wider needle. Cut the end of the wire on a slant to create a point and it should now go through the braid more easily.

2. Push through 2cm of the wire and bend both sides of the wire towards the end of the braid. Twist the two ends together and trim off the shorter end.

3. Thread the cone onto the wire and a bead can be added to decorate the end of the cone. Form a wrapped loop.

4. Attach the clasp with jump rings.

Clasp alternative – making your own wire hook and eye clasp

It is not always possible to find exactly the clasp you want to match a particular braid, but once the wrapped loop technique has been mastered, it is easy to adapt this skill to make your own hook and eye fastening. This can be used with any of the wire methods explained in this chapter. Just remember to allow a longer length of wire.

Additional equipment – looping pliers will make a more even hook than can be made with round-nose pliers.

1. To make the hook end of the clasp, use a 16cm length of wire to attach the cone and bead, as described in the instructions for the wired ending master technique. Grip the wire with the round-nose pliers 3cm from the bead. Bend the wire back on itself.

2. Take the bend in the tip of the pliers and curve it up slightly to shape the end of the hook.

3. Move the looping pliers to the midway point between the bead and the bend and curve the wires into a hook shape. A large knitting needle or a slim pen could be used instead of looping pliers.

4. Grip the wires close to the bead, allowing enough room for a few wraps, and wrap the loose wire around the base of the hook, close to the bead. Use flat-nose pliers to squash down any sharp ends on the wrap. The hook can be manipulated to form a pleasing shape, with just a small opening to allow the other side of the clasp to pass through.

5. To make the eye, use a 12cm length of wire to attach the cone and bead as before. Use the widest part of the round-nose pliers or a medium step on the looping pliers to make a large wrapped loop to accommodate the hook.

Wire cone

Making your own cones out of wire is very convenient and satisfying. The best way to get evenly coiled cones is to use a cone-making tool, such as Wags Wicone or Conetastic. There are several types and sizes available. The easiest to use are those with a hole at the tip of the cone, but those with a hole at the base of the cone are also workable. The tip of the wire cone will be wider than the wrapped loop, so it is necessary to use at least a 4mm bead to cover it.

It is also possible to improvise with a pen top or similarly shaped household item. Making a hole in the top to secure the wire will make it much easier to use.

Materials – wire, 2 x 4mm beads, clasp, 2 jump rings.

Equipment – Wags Wicone or Conetastic.

1. It is hard to judge exactly how much wire is needed, so working from the reel is advised. The cone in the photo required 50cm of wire. Make a small loop approximately 1cm from the end of the wire with round-nose pliers. This is an important step as it makes the cone easy to remove. Insert the end of the wire into the hole in the tool.

2. Turn the tool with one hand, guiding the wire with the other. Make sure you are turning the tool and not wrapping the wire around the tool, because this will twist the wire, making it harder to achieve even coils. Count the coils as you work, so that the second cone can be made to the same size.

3. When the desired size has been achieved, either cut the wire close to the last coil or allow an extra 2cm, which can be formed into a decorative spiral that can be folded either up against the cone or down below it.

4. To remove the cone from the tool, cut the wire at the top, close to the small loop, to release the piece of wire that was inserted into the hole. Snip off the loop.

5. The wire cone can now be used with the instructions for the wired ending master technique. Using a bead to finish it off, and making sure that the wrapped loop is formed close to the bead will ensure that the coils of the cone remain tight. Use pliers to press down the cut end of the wire at the top of the cone so that it does not protrude.

Beaded wire cone

This is a pretty variation on the plain wire cone, which makes a statement feature of the ending. It makes a chunky cone, so it needs to be topped off with a 6–8mm bead.

Materials – wire, beads, 6–8mm bead.

Equipment – Wags Wicone or Conetastic.

1. Thread the beads onto the wire. As before, it is best to work from the reel. It is also hard to judge how many beads are needed, so thread on a generous amount. This cone will require a shorter length of wire than a plain cone. The cones in the photo required 70 beads and 40cm of wire for each cone.

2. Make a small loop approximately 1cm from the end of the wire with round-nose pliers. This is an important step as it makes it easy to remove the cone from the cone-making tool.

3. Insert the end of the wire into the hole and turn the tool with one hand and guide the wire with the other hand to create two complete coils around the tip of the tool.

4. Push the beads close to the coils and continue to turn the tool, feeding the beads onto the cone closely, while guiding the wire to create close coils. Make sure you are turning the tool and not wrapping the wire around the tool, because this will twist the wire, making it harder to achieve even coils.

5. When the cone has reached the desired size, check the beads are all sitting closely together with no gaps. Feed more beads up the wire if necessary. Cut the wire 2–3cm from the last bead and quickly form a small spiral to keep the beads in place.

6. Remove the cone from the tool by cutting the wire close to the loop. Snip off the loop.

7. The beaded cone can now be used with the instructions for the wired ending master technique. Using a bead to finish it off and making sure that the wrapped loop is formed close to the bead will ensure that the coils of the cone remain tight. Use pliers to press down the cut end of the wire at the top of the cone so that it does not protrude.

Wire coil

Wire coils are made in a similar way to the wire cone method, but the end result is slimmer and neater. A length of wire with a spiral at one end is used to pierce the braid. A headpin with a large, decorative head could also be used. It is not essential to use looping pliers/bail-making pliers, but they do make the process easier and come in a choice of sizes. If necessary, knitting needles make a good substitute tool.

Materials – wire, 6–8mm bead.

Equipment – looping pliers/bail-making pliers.

1. Take 12cm of wire and make a small spiral at one end. Pierce the sealed and trimmed braid with the wire, as described in the instructions for the wired ending master technique. Pull the wire right through the braid and press the spiral close to the braid. Bend the wire towards the end of the braid.

2. Select the step on the pliers which is large enough to accommodate the braid and the wire. Working from the reel of wire, grip the end of the wire with the pliers and turn the pliers to make two circles of wire. Remove the wire from the pliers and check that the size is correct by sliding it onto the braid and wire.

3. Return the wire to the pliers and carry on turning the pliers to create a coil that is long enough to cover the braid from the wire spiral to just beyond the end. Remember to turn the pliers, and not to wrap the wire around the pliers, to avoid twisting the wire. Cut the wire close to the coil.

4. Thread the coil onto the wire and the braid. Thread on a bead and finish off with a wrapped loop. Use pliers to press down the cut ends of the wire at both ends of the coil to prevent it catching.

5. Attach the clasp with jump rings. Alternatively, make your own hook fastening.

Beaded sleeve

A basic knowledge of peyote stitch is required for this method. Creating your own beaded sleeve and topping it off with a decorative bead is an excellent way to complete a braid, and it is particularly effective if beadwork is used elsewhere in the design, such as in a beadwork pendant or a beaded bead focal. Flat peyote stitch is a good starting point for this type of ending, but experimenting with other stitches will produce some lovely effects.

Materials – seed beads, beading thread, wire, 2 x 6–8mm round beads, jump rings and clasp.

Equipment – beading needle.

1. Start by piercing the braid with the wire and twisting the ends together as described in steps 1 and 2 for the wired ending master technique.

2. Thread the decorative bead onto the wire and keep it in position with a wrapped loop.

3. Make a rectangle of flat peyote stitch. The number of beads per row depends on the size of the braid. Start with 12 size 11 beads, so that there are six beads for both of the first two rows. Hold it against the braid to check that it looks balanced. If so, continue to add rows until the rectangle is large enough to wrap around the braid. A snug fit is best. Stitch together the sides of the rectangle, so that the braid is covered. Make sure that your thread comes out on the opposite side to the end of the braid.

4. Push the beaded sleeve close to the decorative bead and use the tail of the thread to sew through the braid several times to keep the sleeve in this position. Try to sew just inside the sleeve, so that the stitching remains invisible.

5. Attach the clasp with jump rings.

Big bead

A very decorative ending can be made with large-holed beads. It is possible to find a wide range of beads with holes ranging from 5mm to 10mm, and by combining them with beads it is possible to create your own end cone effect. They are particularly attractive on bracelets and front-fastening necklaces.

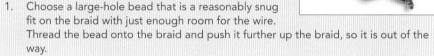

Materials – 2 large-hole beads, 2 6–8mm beads, wire, jump rings and clasp.

1. Choose a large-hole bead that is a reasonably snug fit on the braid with just enough room for the wire. Thread the bead onto the braid and push it further up the braid, so it is out of the way.

2. Pierce the braid with wire as described in the instructions for the wired ending master technique. Push through 2cm and bend it into a U shape.

3. Bring the bead back up the braid so that it covers the wire. Trim the shorter wire so that it is flush with the end of the bead. Trim any protruding braid so that it is also flush with the end of the bead.

4. Thread the decorative bead onto the wire and keep it in position with a wrapped loop.

5. Attach the clasp with jump rings.

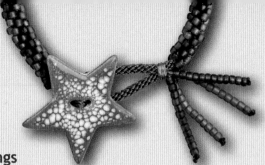

Button fastenings

Button fastenings are a great alternative to using glue or wire to attach a clasp, and they also offer the opportunity to create a really personal look by using vintage, novelty or handmade buttons. There are several different methods of creating a button fastening and it is a good idea to try them all to find your favourite. This type of technique needs to be planned from the beginning because the braid starts with either the button or the loop, rather than the ending being added on after braiding. Double the length of cord and half the number of cords are required when the braiding starts in this way.

Choosing the button

Buttons with either a shank or with holes through the middle can be used, as long as the holes can accommodate the required number of cords. The size of the button is a matter of personal choice, but buttons smaller than 1.5cm can be fiddly to use. Remember that the loop will be visible to approximately half the diameter of the button, so very large buttons will lead to a long length of plain braid being visible.

Cord allowance

The length of cord required for a braided loop will depend on the size of the button and the type of loop. Allowing 10–20cm extra length for each cord will usually suffice, but if you are using very large buttons or are making a braid with thick cords, add more.

Sizing

To calculate the correct length for the braid for a piece of jewellery, allow approximately one and a quarter to one and a half times the diameter of the button for the fastening.

Attaching the weight to the button

If a clip-on weight is being used, it may be possible to clip it directly onto the button. If not, when the cords are in position on the disk, tie a piece of cord around the button, knot the ends of the cord together and clip the weight onto the knot. When the braid is long enough for the button to emerge from under the disk, it will be possible to clip the weight directly onto the braid.

Button alternatives

Although buttons are used in all of these methods, other items, such as toggles or large beads, can be substituted.

Loop and button with binding

By using a discreet binding of thin thread in a matching colour to close a loop of braid, it is easy to achieve a good fit for the button. The braid is made slightly longer than required to allow for adjustments and any excess braid is unravelled after the binding is in place. These instructions are for beaded braids, but they can be used for braids without beads, using ending Method 1.

Materials – 1 button, with or without a shank.

Equipment – darning needle.

1. The braid is set up using the simple start technique. Thread all the cords through the button, hold the button in the middle of the hole in the disk and position the cords in the slots. Braid for eight individual cord moves without beads. If the button has holes through it rather than a shank, braid for approximately 5mm to allow space for the braided loop. Then start to braid with beads and braid to the required length.

2. Continue to braid without beads until this section is long enough to form a loop for the button plus a 5mm allowance for the binding. This will be approximately three times the diameter of the button. Remove the braid from the disk and tie the end in an overhand knot. Give the braid a firm stretch and allow it to relax back into shape.

3. Fold over the braid to form a loop that the button will fit through, allowing for a 5mm binding. Use a needle and thread to join the loop together with a binding, close to the beads. Check that the button will fit through the loop.

4. Undo the knot at the end of the braid and unravel the braid up to the binding.

5. There are two alternative methods of dealing with the cord ends.

6. **Method 1**: To make a 4-strand beaded tassel take two cords and thread 10–16 beads onto both cords. Separate the cords to push the beads close to the binding, but not too close or the tassel will be very rigid. Tie a double knot to keep the beads in place and trim and seal the knots. Repeat for the other cords in pairs. Larger-holed beads may need a triple knot. If smaller-holed beads are used, it may not be possible to pass two cords through the beads, so an 8-strand tassel can be made, finishing off with overhand knots.

7. **Method 2**: To conceal the cord ends, thread one cord through the eye of a darning needle. When beads are braided into Round Braid/Kongo Gumi, a small space is created in the middle of the braid. Pass the needle into this space and bring the needle out further down the braid. Make sure the needle passes between the beads and not through the hole in the bead. Repeat for all the other cords, bringing the needle out in a slightly different place on the braid each time.

8. Trim off the cord ends by pulling firmly, snipping the cord close to the braid and allowing the cut end to retreat back into the braid.

Braided buttonhole 1

Learning this method is an excellent way of extending your braiding skills. The buttonhole is made using Ladder Braid/ Shippou, which is a type of 8-cord braid, so it can be used together with any braid made with eight cords. It is a good idea to practise the braid first, so that you can braid confidently and accurately before you embark on a design.

Materials – 1 button, with or without a shank.

1. The braid is set up using the simple start technique. Thread all the cords through the button, hold the button in the middle of the hole and position the cords on the disk. Braid for at least eight individual cord moves before adding beads. If the button has holes through it rather than a shank, braid for 5mm to allow space for the braided loop. Continue to braid to the required length. Stop braiding when the cords are on either side of the dots in the north, south, east and west positions on the disk.

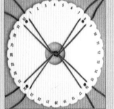

2. Turn the disk so that the cords are in an X shape, with slot 1 to the left. The two pairs of cords on the left will now be worked separately from the two pairs on the right, and a hole will form in the middle of the braid.

3. Start with the 8 cords on the left side of the disk and ignore all the other cords. Move the top-left cord to the bottom right, and move the cord to its left to the top left.

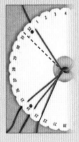

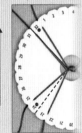

4. Move the top-right cord to the bottom left and move the cord to its right to the top right.

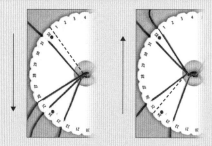

5. Move the bottom two cords back to either side of the dot. The disk now looks the same as the set-up.
6. Now work the cords on the right side of the disk, which will be the mirror image of the moves already performed.
7. Move the top-right cord to the bottom left and move the cord to its right to the top right.

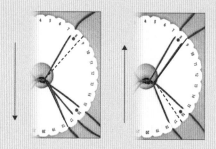

8. Move the top-left cord to the bottom right and move the cord to its left to the top left.

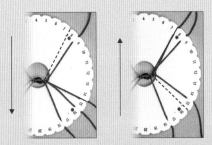

9. Move the bottom two cords back to either side of the dot. The disk now looks the same as the set-up.

10. Repeat the moves on both sides of the disk in turn. A hole will form in the middle. Continue the moves until the hole is big enough for the button to slide through.

11. Return the disk to the usual position, with the dots in the north, south, east and west positions. Pinch the two sides of the braid together from underneath the disk and resume braiding using Round Braid/Kongo Gumi. The first few moves will seem a little loose, but the braid will tighten up once all eight cords have been moved. Braid for 2cm.

12. Remove the braid from the disk and tie the end of the braid in a fairly loose overhand knot. Use thread in a matching colour to create a neat binding close to the buttonhole.

13. Untie the loose knot and undo the braid up to the binding. Take two cords and tie them together in an overhand knot approximately 2cm from the binding. Thread several beads onto both cords, separate the cords and tie a double knot. Trim and seal the knots.

Plaited buttonhole

This method is a simplified version of Braided buttonhole 1. Instead of braiding, simple plaiting is used to construct the buttonhole. The two sides of the buttonhole can either be joined in a knot or they can be joined with a binding. For thicker cords a binding is the neatest option.

Materials – button, with or without a shank.

1.   The braid is set up using the simple start technique. Thread all the cords through the button, hold the button in the middle of the hole and position the cords on the disk. Braid to the required length.

2.   Lift two opposite cords from the disk and tie them in a double knot. Remove the braid from the disk.

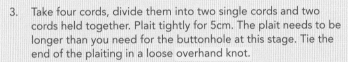

3.   Take four cords, divide them into two single cords and two cords held together. Plait tightly for 5cm. The plait needs to be longer than you need for the buttonhole at this stage. Tie the end of the plaiting in a loose overhand knot.

4.   Repeat the plaiting for the other four cords. Bind the two plaits together allowing a hole for the button to pass through. Alternatively, the plaits can be tied together in an overhand knot to create the hole for the button. Untie the knots at the end of the plaits and unravel the plaiting up to the binding or knot.

5.   Trim the cord ends to make a neat tassel and seal the cord ends to prevent fraying. Alternatively, beads can be added to the end of the tassel and secured with an overhand knot, or metal crimp covers can be closed over the cord ends for a decorative effect.

Braided buttonhole 2

In this variation the buttonhole is made at the beginning of the braid. In these instructions 8-cord round braid/kongo gumi is used for the loop and the braid is brought together to form a 16-cord braid. The loop always requires half the number of cords used for the main part of the design, so other combinations can be used, such as a 6-cord hollow braid with a 12-cord round braid.

Materials – a button with a shank is required for this technique.

1. Start with 8 double length cords. The cords need to be tied together in an off-centre knot. Fold the cords in half. Measure 15cm from the fold and tie a loose overhand knot at this point. The knot will be untied later, so do not make it too tight.

2. Position the longer cords on the disk and wrap the shorter cords on a bobbin to hang on the underside of the disk. Braid to create enough length to form a loop to accommodate the button, making sure that the braid has been stretched and allowed to relax back into shape for 10 minutes before the final decision on length is made.

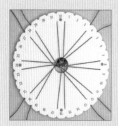

3. Unwind the cords from the bobbin, undo the knot and bring the cords through the hole in the disk from underneath, one pair into each quarter of the disk. Position the cords in pairs so that they are equally spaced around the disk.

4. Braid for 16 individual cord moves, making sure that the cords are pulled up firmly to join the two braids into one. Continue to braid to the required length. For a beaded braid, allow enough braid without beads for the button to sit flat on the braid.

5. Lift one cord and thread it through the loop on the button. Replace the cord in its slot. Lift the next cord and thread it through the loop, replacing it in its slot afterwards. Do the same for as many cords as will fit through, up to half the total number of cords. Press the button close to the point of braiding and keep it below the cords on the disk.

6. Continue to braid for 1cm. This will trap the button in the braid. Remove the braid from the disk and bind the braid tightly close to the button. Trim the cord ends to form a tassel. Most cords can be unravelled to create a fuller tassel, but check first on a piece of scrap cord.

Variation: Make a longer length of braid at the beginning and create the loop by tying the braid in an overhand knot. Unravel any excess braid and position the cords on the disk with the knot in the middle. Continue with the instructions above from step 4. This is a very straightforward way of getting the fit correct.

Beaded loop and button

A beaded loop is a very pretty way of making a feature of the fastening. It is possible either to start with the button or start with the loop, so both options are provided.

Method 1 – Starting with the button

Before you start, make sure that you can thread four cords through the beads you intend to use. It may be a snug fit, but stiffening the cords and threading them through one by one may help.

Materials – button with or without a shank, size 6 beads.

1. The braid is set up using the simple start technique. Thread all the cords through the button, hold the button in the middle of the hole in the disk and position the cords in the slots. Braid for eight individual cord moves without beads. If the button has holes through it rather than a shank, braid for approximately 5mm to allow space for the beaded loop.

2. Braid with beads to the required length. Then braid without beads for approximately eight moves.

3. Lift two opposite cords from the disk and tie them together in a double knot tight against the end of the braid. This is enough to stop the braid from unravelling, so the braid can be removed from the disk.

4. Thread 4 cords through 8–14 size 6 beads. Thread the other 4 cords through 8–14 size 6 beads. Tie the cords together loosely using a double knot to check that the size is correct for the button. Retie the cords tightly when you are satisfied that the size is correct.

5. Use the cord ends to make a tassel. Take two cords and tie them together in an overhand knot approximately 2cm from the beaded loop. Thread several beads onto both cords, separate the cords and tie a double knot. Trim and seal the knots.

Method 2 – Starting with the loop

Materials – a button with a shank is best for this technique, crimp covers (optional).

1. Thread two or more cords through as many beads as are needed to create a large enough loop for the button to fit through. Using an odd number of beads creates the best loop. There is no stretch in this type of loop, so do not make it too small. Centre the beads on the cords and tie the cords into a circle using a double knot. Check that the button fits the loop.

2. Hold the bead loop in the middle of the hole in the disk and position the cords on the disk. Lay any extra cords that would not fit through the beads across the disk in their slots.

3. Braid for at least eight moves before adding beads. The additional cords will be woven into the braid.

4. Braid to the required length. If making a beaded braid, now braid for eight further moves without beads. Lift one cord from its slot and thread it through the button. Replace it in its slot to retain the tension of the braid. Repeat for up to three more cords.

5. Remove the braid from the disk and tie the button tightly against the braid with a double knot.

6. There are two methods for dealing with the cord ends. For a fully beaded Round Braid/ Kongo Gumi, the cords can be concealed in the small space in the middle of the braid. Thread one cord into a darning needle and pass the needle into the space, bringing the needle out further down the braid. Make sure the needle passes between the beads and not through the hole in the bead.

7. Repeat for the other cords, bringing them out in slightly different places each time. Trim off the cord ends by pulling firmly on the cord, cutting it close to the braid and allowing the cut end to retreat into the braid. After all the cords have been concealed, a drop of glue can be added to the knot under the button for extra security.

8. For other types of braid, the cords can be made into a tassel. First tie all the cords in an overhand knot and press the knot as close to the previous knot and the button as possible. Take two cords and tie them in an overhand knot at the point where the tassel should end. Trim and seal the knot. While the glue is still tacky, push the knot into a crimp cover. Use pliers to close the cover so that it grips the cords. Crimp covers can be fiddly to close, but the glue will help to keep it in place while you press it closed with pliers. Repeat for all the cords.

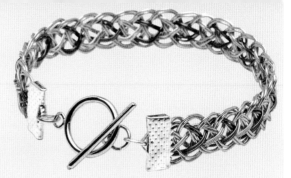

Crimp endings

This chapter concentrates on the sort of findings that can be squeezed or folded to grip or clamp the braid. There are many different types of crimp endings and they can be described in several different ways depending on what materials they were designed to be used with, for example ribbon clamp and leather crimp. A separate clasp is usually attached to the crimp ending with jump rings. For all of these findings the braid needs to be sealed with glue first. It is best to attach the crimp ending as soon as the glue is touch-dry, so that when the crimp ending is squeezed, the braid will also be compressed, forming a really firm bond.

Master technique for ribbon endings

Ribbon endings are particularly useful for flat braids and they come in many different widths. They fold over the end of the braid and grip it tightly. Some have teeth for a firmer hold. They often feature a patterned surface to hide any pressure marks made by pliers. Nylon-nose pliers can be used to minimise damage. This type of ending can be used without glue, but for a secure hold and to assist in the positioning of the braid, glue is recommended. Strong glue may be used, although all-purpose glue will be strong enough because it is used as a backup to the crimp ending.

Materials – crimp endings.

Equipment – flat-nose or chain-nose pliers, nylon-nose pliers (optional).

1. Assess the depth of the finding and carefully trim the sealed braid to fit, making sure that the glued section will be covered.

2. Apply a small amount of glue to the cut end of the braid and press it firmly into the fold of the ribbon ending. Do not use too much glue, because when pressure is applied to the finding in the next step, excess glue may squeeze out at the sides. Allow the glue to dry but not harden.

3. Use pliers to press the middle of the finding together fairly gently, so that the metal is touching the braid on both sides. Press each end of the finding in the same manner in turn. Check that the braid is still in the correct position and then exert greater pressure, first in the middle and then at the ends, so that the braid is firmly gripped.

4. Turn the pliers to the side of the braid and press the sides firmly together, one after the other.

5. Use jump rings to attach a clasp.

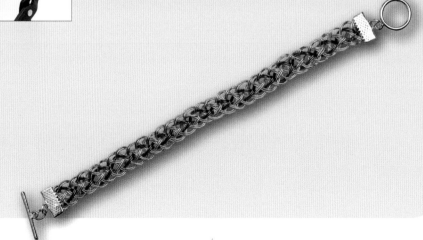

Ribbon ending for wire braids

This type of ending is particularly effective for wire kumihimo.

1. Wire kumihimo does not unravel in the way cord does, so it is not necessary to seal the end of the braid with glue. Assess the depth of the finding and cut across the end of the braid to create a really straight end.
2. Use strong glue to secure the wire in the ending to help you to keep the braid in the desired position while you close up the end with pliers. Close up the ribbon ending as described in the master technique for ribbon endings. Squashing the braid may make the individual wires spread out slightly, so work slowly, paying attention to any stray wires protruding from the sides and tucking them back in before proceeding.

Multiple braid ending

1. For a 3-braid plaited design, start with the three braids sealed and trimmed at one end. Glue the braids into the ending, side by side, using strong glue or all-purpose glue, and then close the end with pliers as described in the master technique for ribbon endings.
2. Plait the three braids together. The tension of this plaiting will affect the length of the bracelet. Tighter plaiting will produce a shorter braid and looser plaiting will produce a longer braid. When you are happy with the effect and the length of the plaiting, secure the end of the plait with a peg. At the ends, glue the braids into the second ending as described in the master technique for ribbon endings.

Side-folding cord endings

These endings need to be folded over twice to secure the braid. They are relatively inexpensive and if they are used correctly, they are very secure. They are usually only available in smaller sizes and, for the best effect, it is important not to overfill them. This type of finding will flatten the braid, which may not be to everyone's taste.

1. Start with sealed braids. The glued section needs to be covered by the finding and the braid should not protrude from the upper edge of the parts that are folded over. Trim the end of the braid to fit.

2. Apply a small amount of glue to the central panel of the finding. Lay the braid on the glue and allow it to set, but not harden.

3. Use pliers to fold over one side of the finding, using multiple small squeezes to bring the side slowly into position. Once that side is in position, press down more firmly so that the braid is gripped.

4. When you are happy with the first side, you can press down the second side, again using multiple small movements, rather than squashing it down quickly in one go.

Cord end crimps

This type of cord ending is commonly used for leather or ready-made cord, but they are also perfect for kumihimo because they are very small and neat. They tend to be available only in the narrower widths, so they are best used for beaded kumihimo made with beading cord. They are usually used with a clasp, but some types do have an integrated hook and eye clasp. The middle section is designed to be flattened with pliers to grip the cord. Securing the braid with glue first is advisable to ensure that the cord position does not shift while you are closing the middle section. You will require pliers with fairly narrow tips because the crimp part of the finding is not very wide, especially for the smaller sizes.

1. Cut the sealed end of the braid to the correct length, making sure that the glued part will be covered by the cord ending. The cord should be positioned so that it is flush with the other end of the finding. If it is protruding from the other end, it is difficult to get scissors in close enough to remove the excess.

2. Use a cocktail stick to apply a very small amount of glue to the part of the braid that will be covered by the cord ending, on the sides only. You need only use enough glue to hold the braid in place as using too much will cause glue to be squeezed out when pressure is applied. Insert the braid into the cord ending, using a twisting motion to spread the glue. Allow it to set but not dry hard, as this will make the crimp section very difficult to close.

3. Use pliers to squeeze the crimp section gently first from one side and then from the other, gradually increasing the pressure until the cord is firmly gripped.

Loop fastenings

Loops of different sorts can make very attractive and unusual fastenings. As these methods make use of the braid or the cord to form the fastening, they tend to be a very cost-effective way of finishing off a piece of jewellery, but they also create a very stylish effect that can be used as the central feature of a design. The length of braid required to form a loop will vary depending on the width of the braid, so allow plenty when working with thicker cords. The wire used in all of the designs is 0.8mm/20 gauge, but a variety of thick-nesses and types of wire could be used, because they do not need to be particularly strong to be used for wrapping techniques. The amount of wire required can vary considerably, so the quantities given here are approximate.

Loop and double toggle fastening

Making a fastening using braided loops is a very versatile and effective method. The double toggle operates like a cufflink, but an S-hook or ribbon tied in a bow would work in the same way.

Materials – wire, 2 toggle bars, 3–4 jump rings.

1. Approximately 8–10cm of braid is required at each end of the design for this type of fastening, depending on the thickness of the braid. Seal the end of the braid with glue. Allow the glue to set but not harden, and cut through the braid at a 45 degree angle.

2. Bend the braid round to form a loop that is just large enough for the toggle to pass through. Use strong thread to bind the join together tightly. Keep the binding narrow because it needs to be covered by the wire. Seal the binding with glue. Alternatively, the join can be stuck together with glue instead of using a binding. Use a peg to hold the join together while the glue dries.

3. Cut 25cm of wire and make a mark 5cm from the end. Use pliers to form a flat spiral at one end, stopping when the mark is reached.

4. Hold the spiral on the join in the braid, with the spiral closest to the loop, and wind the wire around the binding five to seven times to cover it. Do not pull the wire too tightly because this can result in an uneven effect. Cut the wire 4cm from the braid and form a smaller spiral. Reduce the wire length and spiral size for narrower braids. Repeat for the other end of the braid.

5. Join two toggles with three jump rings and use them to join the loops of braid. The number of jump rings used can be adjusted to create a close connection.

Double bracelet loop fastening

This bracelet combines a loop with other techniques, by folding a double-length braid in half and then threading on a large-hole bead to form a loop. An end cone and toggle are attached to the other end using the wired method, but the glue method could be used, if preferred. A wire coil could be used instead of the bead.

Materials – wire, toggle, cone, bead, jump ring, large-hole bead to fit double the thickness of the braid.

1. Take a double-length braid and fold it in half. Thread the large-hole bead onto the fold in the braid to create a loop that is large enough to allow the toggle to pass through. The bead needs to be a snug fit on the braid, and if this is the case, a binding is not necessary. If it is not a snug fit, bind the two braids together to create the loop and add as much binding thread as necessary to keep the bead in place. Seal the binding with glue.

2. For the other end of the bracelet, use thread to bind the two braid ends together. Add a drop of glue to the binding for extra security.

3. Cut 10cm of wire and pass 2cm of wire in between the two braids on the inside of the binding. Twist the wire together and trim off the shorter end. Thread on a cone and a bead and keep them in place with a wrapped loop. Attach a toggle with a jump ring.

Loop and toggle

This method makes use of the cord as a loop and the toggle is worked into the braid. You could substitute a button or a wire hook for the toggle. The braid is set up using a variation of the simple start technique, so the cords need to be double length, but you only need half as many cords.

Materials – toggle bar from a toggle clasp.

1. To form the loop, one cord needs to be 10cm longer than the rest. Find the mid-point of the longer cord and form a loop by tying an overhand knot. Check that the toggle will pass through the loop and then tighten the knot.

2. Hold the loop in the middle of the hole in the disk and position the ends of the cord in slots 1 and 17, so that they are diagonally opposite. Centre the remaining cords on the disk, using diagonally opposite slots. Braid for eight individual cord moves, starting with the knotted cord. The loose cords will be worked into the braid. Continue to braid to the required length.

3. Lift one cord from the disk and thread it through the toggle. Replace the cord in its slot. Repeat for half the cords, one by one. If they will not all fit, thread through as many as possible. Push the toggle as close to the braid as possible and push it under the cords on the disk.

4. Continue to braid for 2cm. Lift two opposite cords and tie them in a loose double knot. This will be undone later, so do not pull it too tight. The braid is now secured sufficiently to remove it from the disk.

5. Use a needle and thread to bind the braid approximately 5mm from the toggle. When securing the thread in the braid at the beginning and end of the binding, make sure that this is done on the braid side and not the tassel side of the binding. Seal the binding with glue.

6. Undo the knot at the end of the braid and undo the braid up to the binding.

7. Decide how long the tassel should be and trim each cord to this length. If the cords are likely to fray or unravel, they can be sealed with a drop of glue. Synthetic cords can be sealed with a cord burner or a naked flame.

Half cuff bracelet and loop

Different styles of half cuff bracelet findings are available, but the features they share are a glue-in section at one end and either a hook or button at the other end. They are perfect for kumihimo because a braid can be folded in half to create a loop to attach to the hook or button.

Materials – half cuff/bangle finding.

1. Make a braid measuring approximately 35cm. Fold the braid in half and tie an overhand knot to create a loop at the end. Check that the loop is the correct size for the hook or button. Tighten the knot, pressing down on it with your thumb to form a neat, flat knot.
2. Check the length of the bracelet and stick the other ends into the glue-in section, using the instructions in the chapter on glued endings.

Beaded half cuff bracelet

1. This bracelet is made of one double-length beaded braid with a bead-free section in the centre for attaching the hook or button. The braid is joined with a double spiral and wrap. The central section used to form the loop needs to be approximately 6cm long, but this depends on the thickness of the braid and the size of the hook or button. Each beaded section needs to be 8–12cm, with thicker braids needing to be longer than thinner braids.

2. Fold the braid in half and cut 15cm of wire. Make a mark 3cm from the end. Use pliers to form a flat spiral at one end, stopping when the mark is reached.
3. Hold the spiral on the braids between the fold and the beads and check that the position of the spiral will allow the button or hook to pass through the loop. Wrap the wire around the two braids two or three times. Do not pull the wire too tightly because this can result in an uneven effect. Cut the wire 3cm from the braid and form a spiral to match the first one.
4. Check the length of the bracelet and stick the other ends into the glue-in section of the finding, using the instructions in the chapter on glued endings.

Tassels

Not all braids need to be finished with a clasp or fastening.
Sometimes a braid may be made as a sample or demonstration piece,
so is not intended for wear, but it still needs to look complete. Long braids
may be made for use as lariats, so they will be tied rather than fastened, and
attaching a tassel at each end of the braid can be very attractive. Other braids
may be used on key rings, bag dangles, bookmarks or as pendants. The aim of
constructing tassels is not to hide or remove the cord ends, but to make them
look attractive.

For the three designs in this chapter the braid is not secured with glue or a knot
when it is removed from the disk, because this would interfere with the formation
of a neat knot or binding. Care needs to be taken to prevent the braid from unravelling.
Either keep the end of the braid firmly gripped between your thumb and forefinger or
clamp it with a peg or clip and only remove it just before the binding or knot is worked.

Tassel at both ends

*Equipment – darning needle (a folded length of wire or cord could be used instead of a
needle).*

1. Decide how long you want your tassel to be, then gather all the cords together and tie
    them in a loose overhand knot, allowing enough cord for the tassel. This knot will be
    undone later, so do not make it too tight.

2. Position the cords on the disk so that the longer cords are in the slots and the shorter
    cords are hanging below the disk. Braid to the required length. Remove the braid from
    the disk, keeping the braid pinched between the thumb and forefinger so that it does
    not unravel.

3. Hold the needle against the braid with the eye on the last part of the braided section. Pull one cord away from the rest. Wrap the cord around the end of the braided section, keeping the needle inside this binding. Start to bind the braid 1–2mm from the end of the braid and bind up the braid towards the middle, not down towards the loose cords. The binding should consist of at least seven wraps, but can be more.

4. Use your thumb or a peg to keep a firm grip on the binding to prevent it from loosening. Thread the binding cord through the eye of the needle and pull the needle out of the binding, bringing the cord under the binding. If the cord has been wrapped very tightly, use pliers to grip the needle.

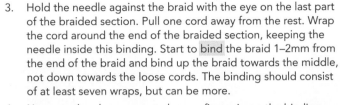

5. Trim the cord ends to the desired length. If cords with multiple strands are being used, they can be untwisted and separated to create a luxuriant tassel. If the cord ends have become curly, they can be straightened by steaming. To do this, give the cords a few blasts of steam from a steam iron, attach a kumihimo weight to the ends and hang the braid up for 10 minutes.

6. Untie the knot at the other end and repeat. The bindings need to be tight to stay in position. A drop of glue can be added for extra security and this is particularly advised for smooth or slippery cords.

Knot and tassel

This is a very quick and easy method of finishing off a braid. It does not allow for a clasp to be attached, so it is perfect for key rings, bag dangles or bookmarks. It is also a neat way of finishing off a pendant.

1. Attach the cords to the finding using the simple start technique and braid to the required length plus an extra 1cm.

2. Pinch the end of the braid between the thumb and forefinger from underneath the disk. Remove the braid from the disk and tie a loose overhand knot. Ease the knot into the required position, tightening it as you move it. If it is a beaded braid, the knot needs to be as close as possible to the beads. Check that you are happy with the knot and retie it if necessary. Once the knot is where you want it, tighten it up fully by pulling

on each individual cord, so that the knot is as small and tight as possible. The knot can be secured with glue, if required.

3. Trim the cords to the desired length for the tassel. If you are using cords with multiple strands, the tassel can be made fuller by unravelling the cords. For twisted cords, such as beading cord, roll the cord between your fingers to loosen the twist and use a needle to tease the individual fibres apart, starting at the end of the cord. These cords are usually made up of three individually twisted bundles of fibres. They can be unravelled either to divide into these three bundles or further to separate the individual fibres. Not all cords can be treated in this way, so check on a scrap length of cord first. Most satin cords and cords of similar construction can only be unravelled in one direction, and those that cannot be unravelled can be trimmed close to the sealed knot.

Clasp and tassel

This is a very useful variation of the knot and tassel method. All you need is a clasp.

Materials – clasp.

1. Attach the cords to the clasp using the simple start technique. If using a toggle clasp, the toggle part should be used here. Braid to the required length.

2. Lift one cord from the disk and thread on the other part of the clasp. Return the cord to its slot. Lift the next cord and thread it through the clasp, then return the cord to its slot. Repeat for as many cords as will fit through the clasp, up to half the cords on the disk. Press the clasp close to the braid.

3. Braid for a further 1cm. Remove the braid from the disk and tie an overhand knot, making sure that you catch the end of the braided part in the knot. Tighten the knot fully by pulling on each individual cord, so that the knot is as small and tight as possible. The knot can be secured with glue, if required.

4. Take two cords and tie them in an overhand knot approximately 1–2cm from the end of the braid, depending on how long you want the tassel to be. Thread several beads onto both cords. Separate the cords and tie a double knot. Seal and trim the cord ends. Repeat for the other cords.

Frequently asked questions

The braid has already been made and it is too long. How can I shorten it?

Bind the braid tightly with thread and add a drop of glue to the binding. Unravel the excess braid up to the binding and remove any beads. Plait the loose cords as tightly as possible and seal the plaiting with glue. Trim the plaited section to the length required to finish off the braid.

The unravelled braid is very curly. How can I straighten it?

Give the cords a few blasts of steam from a steam iron. Attach a weight to the bottom of the cords and hang the braid up for 10 minutes.

The braid has already been made without the button on the end, but I want a button fastening. How do I do that?

Either use a small glue-on end cap and a jump ring to attach the button, or seal the braid 2cm from the end with a spot of glue and unravel the braid up to the glue. Thread the button onto half the cords and tie it on using a double knot. Trim the cord ends close to the knot and seal with glue.

The braided loop has stretched. What do I do?

Pinch the end of the loop into a tight bend and bind it with matching thread. This will be hidden under the button when in use.

How do I make the necklace adjustable in length?

Make extra braid and use the same type of clasp at each end, so that it can be joined to the necklace as an extender. Alternatively, use a clasp with a length of extension chain attached.

How can a 7-cord braid be used with a button start?

Start with eight cords and put two cords together in one slot. Braid as usual, with the two cords in the same slot worked together as one cord. After braiding for 1cm, the extra cord can be trimmed close to the braid.

I am allergic to metal. How can I avoid metal in my endings?

Using button fastenings is the easiest way to avoid metal. Buttons can be made of so many different materials such as wood, ceramic, plastic, bone and shell, so there is no shortage of choice. Alternatively, try the loop and double toggle fastening on page 61, using just a binding without the wire spirals and join the loops with a length of ribbon.

Where can I find instructions for the jewellery designs shown in this book?

It depends on the complexity of the design. The more complex designs are available as tutorials on the Prumihimo® website (Prumihimo.com). Less complex designs have been filmed as videos for the Prumihimo® YouTube channel (YouTube.com/c/Prumihimo).

How can I make a cone for use with wired endings?

You can use 2-hole dagger beads to make a very attractive cone. Simply take five 2-hole dagger beads and sew through the top hole of each bead. Pass through all the holes several times to make a firm connection. Sew through the middle holes and tighten the thread to create a cone shape. Sew through the middle holes several times until the cone holds its shape. Attach the cone as described on page 32 and finish off with a 4mm round bead.

How can I use a magnetic clasp without using the glued ending?

Use the clasp and tassel method on page 69. A safety chain, as described on page 27, could be added for extra security.

Can I use the wired ending for a flat braid?

Yes you can, but as the majority of cones are either round or oval you will need to roll the end of the braid and bind it to make it fit the cone.

What are the best ways to finish beaded braids made with very fine thread?

Either of the beaded buttonhole techniques on pages 50 and 51 work well with very thin braids. If you wish to use a clasp use the clasp and tassel instructions on page 69.

Which ending method should I use if I wish my jewellery to be washable?

If a piece of jewellery is likely to need frequent washing it is best to use a button fastening, using a washable button and a fray prevention product to seal any knots or bindings. Other types of ending will tolerate a few quick and gentle washes as long as the item is dried without delay in a warm, but not hot, place. The best glues to use for a washable finish are 2-part epoxy and fray prevention products.

Measurements and conversions

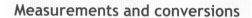

Metric	Imperial
1–2mm	1/16in
3–4mm	1/8in
5–6mm	1/4in
7–8mm	5/16in
9mm–1cm	3/8in
1.5cm	5/8in
2cm	3/4in
3cm	1 1/8in
4cm	1 1/2in
5cm	2in
6cm	2 3/8in

Metric	Imperial
7cm	2 3/4in
8cm	3 1/8in
9cm	3 1/2in
10cm	4in
15cm	5 3/4in
20cm	8in
25cm	9 7/8in
30cm	12in
40cm	15 5/8in
50cm	20in

The measurements in this book use the metric system. When measuring cord or wire it is not necessary to be precise, so this conversion table gives an approximate value.

The measurements for end caps do need to be precise. They are usually sold worldwide using the metric measurements. To check the diameter of a braid, put it on the end of the metric ruler and look down from directly above.

0cm 1 2 3 4 5 6 7 8 9 10 11 12

0in 1/2 1 1 1/2 2 2 1/2 3 3 1/2 4 4 1/2

These printed rulers are provided for quick reference, but for greater accuracy, please use a ruler or tape measure.

About the author

Pru McRae's lifelong love of jewellery and jewellery making led her to the wonderful Japanese art of kumihimo braiding. From the first time she picked up a kumihimo disk she was totally hooked and wanted to share her new passion with others. Her first opportunity came when she was asked to write tutorials for a UK magazine and she enjoyed this so much that she decided to set up her own website to provide a more comprehensive range of instructions and tutorials. This brought her to the attention of the wider jewellery-making community and she was invited to be a guest designer on a jewellery shopping channel.

Regular appearances on the show soon meant that she was being asked to teach in person at workshops. She found that teaching was not only extremely enjoyable, but also that it enabled her to understand the needs of braiders. So, in 2015 she developed her own design of the kumihimo disk, the Prumihimo® disk, to simplify a traditional Japanese braid structure, which allowed braiders to develop their skills. Its success encouraged her to write her first book in 2016, *The Prumihimo® Disk: A fresh approach to kumihimo*. *Kumihimo Endings: The finishing touch for every braid* has been written in response to frequent requests for comprehensive instructions on how to turn braids into jewellery, by way of effective and imaginative endings.

Pru's aim is to use modern methods and materials to push the boundaries of what is possible with kumihimo braiding and to share her innovative and creative approach with a wider audience. To enable this she continues to write for magazines, teach, demonstrate, film videos for YouTube (YouTube.com/c/Prumihimo) and she also has plans for several more books.

Be sure to keep an eye out for her and her classes by visiting her website: Prumihimo.com